RAYS

SEA MONSTERS

HOMER SEWARD

The Rourke Press, Inc.
Vero Beach, Florida 32964

PHOTO CREDITS
All photos © Marty Snyderman

EDITORIAL SERVICES:
Penworthy Learning Systems

Library of Congress Cataloging-in-Publication Data

Seward, Homer. 1942-
   Rays / by Homer Seward.
      p. cm. — (Sea monsters)
   Includes index
   Summary: Introduces the unusually shaped fish called rays, describing their physical appearance, types, where they live, their habits, and prey.
   ISBN 1-57103-239-8
   1. Rays (Fishes)—Juvenile literature. [1. Rays (Fishes)]   I. Title.
II. Series: Seward, Homer, 1942-   Sea monsters.
QL638.8.S48 1998
597.3'5—dc21   98–20297
                                                               CIP
                                                               AC

Printed in the USA

TABLE OF CONTENTS

SKATES AND RAYS

Most skates and rays look like saucers with tails, but they are fish with an unusual shape. Skates are a type of ray.

Rays have skeletons made of **cartilage** (KAHR ti lij). Cartilage also forms the bridge of your nose. Cartilage is rather stiff, but it can bend. Most fish have skeletons of bone.

Rays are generally harmless to people. Some have weapons, though, that are frightening.

With flaps of its flat body, a southern stingray glides along the sandy sea bottom.

RAYS AS SEA MONSTERS

Even the most frightening fish aren't sea monsters, whether they are rays or some other fish. Sea monsters are make-believe.

Long ago, some of the biggest rays were called monsters. Even now some of the big rays are known as "devilfish."

Forward-facing fins that look like horns earned this ray the nickname "devilfish."

A bullseye electric ray rests on the sea bottom.

There is nothing monster-like about smaller rays, except for their weapons. Some **species** (SPEE sheez), or kinds, make their own electricity. They can give a powerful shock.

Certain stingrays and some manta rays have spines on their backs or tails. Those weapons can cause bloody, burning wounds.

WHAT RAYS LOOK LIKE

Usually, a ray has two fins, like little sails, on its tail. Many rays have an opening behind each eye. These are **spiracles** (SPIR uh kulz). A ray sucks water through its spiracles. It releases water through five **gill** (GIL) openings on the lower side of its body.

Rays can be pizza-size or a whopping 20 feet (6 meters) across. The biggest weigh up to 4,000 pounds (about 1800 kilograms). Guitarfish are rays shaped like guitars.

White underbelly of this southern stingray shows its mouth and five gills on each side.

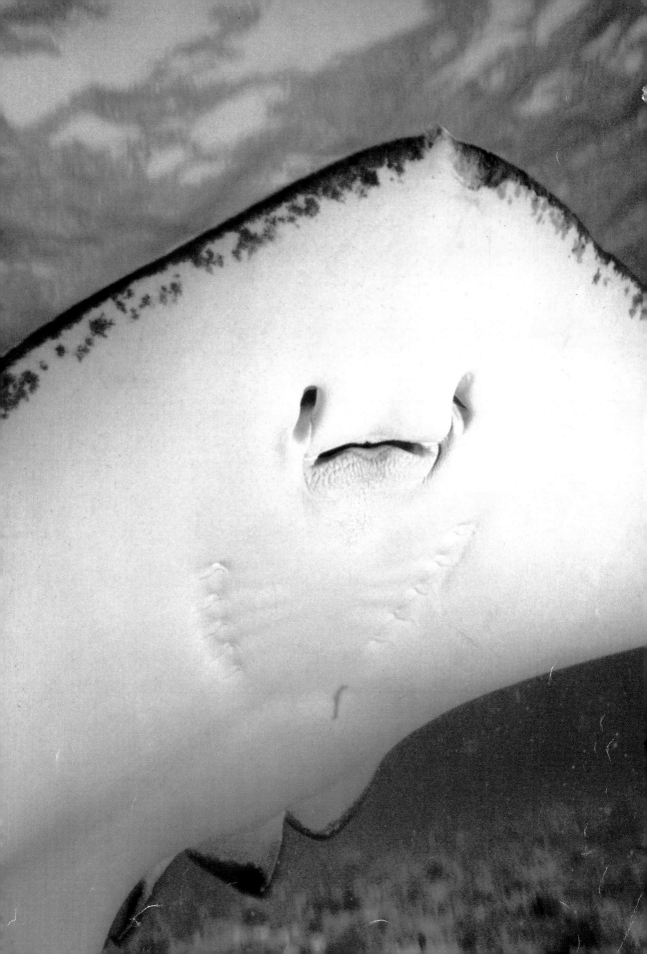

WHERE RAYS LIVE

Rays are mostly **marine** (muh REEN), or ocean-going, fish. They live in all oceans, in deep and shallow water.

A few species live in fresh water and **brackish** (BRAK ish) water. Brackish water is a mix of fresh and salt water.

The electric rays live only in warm seas. The famous mantas and devil rays are found in the eastern Atlantic Ocean and western Mediterranean Sea.

Many rays live in the sandy shallows at the sea's edge. That's where swimmers can step on them.

Rays live in a variety of ocean homes throughout the world. Some live at ocean depths of nearly two miles (three kilometers).

HABITS OF RAYS

Rays swim by flapping their wide, flat bodies. A swimming manta or eagle ray might remind you of a bird beating its wings.

Rays are **predators** (PRED uh turz), or hunters. They feed on other marine animals, including tiny floating animals called **plankton** (PLANGK ton).

Spine of a stingray can cause a painful, bloody wound. The spine sometimes breaks off in the wound.

This manta ray sifts plankton from the ocean.

Many of the common American stingrays eat fish, worms, and clams.

A stingray can swing its tail in any direction to defend itself. A large stingray can drive its tail spike through the side of a wooden boat!

KINDS OF RAYS

Scientists have named about 350 species of rays in 17 groups. One of the most interesting rays is the sawfish. It has a ray's flat body. It also has a long snout with rows of long, sharp teeth. A big sawfish can weigh 5,000 pounds (2,270 kilograms).

Also interesting is the electric ray family with some 35 species. The largest of these super-charged fish is about 5 feet (one and a half meters) long and 174 pounds (80 kilograms).

At a safe distance, this diver films an electric ray.

MANTA RAYS

The Atlantic manta ray is the largest of the rays, at 22 feet (nearly 7 meters) across. The Atlantic manta can be quite frightening.

The big manta doesn't have a spine on its tail. Still, if hooked or harpooned, its size alone makes it dangerous to people or small boats.

The manta, like a giant flying carpet, sometimes leaps from the water. It falls back with a loud smack.

Mantas feed on small fish and plankton, which they suck into their wide mouths.

Manta ray dwarfs the diver trailing below.

THE RAY'S COUSINS

The ray's cousins are sharks. Like rays, sharks also have skeletons of cartilage.

Several species of sharks and rays look like combinations of the two groups. Guitarfish, for example, have the flat heads and upper bodies of rays. Their mid and rear sections, though, are more shark-like.

Band Guitarfish looks like a mix of ray and other fish with raised back fins.

Shark, ray, or mystery fish? Despite the almost-flat body, Australia's spotted wobbegong is a shark.

Sawfish, too, are partly flat and partly round, like sharks. The dorsal, or back, fins of guitarfish and sawfish are triangles, like shark fins.

RAYS AND PEOPLE

People have found rays both useful and dangerous. Many species of rays are caught by fishermen to be sold for food.

In parts of Africa and Asia, people used stingray spines as weapons and ray tails as whips.

A wound caused by a stingray spine and its poison is painful. Stingray wounds are not likely to kill anyone, but they can be deadly if they're in a person's stomach.

This diver swims with a manta ray. No one inexperienced with large fish should approach one.

GLOSSARY

brackish (BRAK ish) — water that is a mix of salt and fresh, such as the water in the mouths of coastal rivers

cartilage (KAHR ti lij) — the strong, flexible body tissue that makes up most of a ray or shark skeleton

gills (GILZ) — the organ that help fish and certain other animals breath by taking oxygen from the water

marine (muh REEN) — of or relating to the ocean

plankton (PLANGK ton) — tiny, floating plants and animals of the sea and other bodies of water

predator (PRED uh tur) — an animal that hunts other animals for food

species (SPEE sheez) — within a group of closely related animals, one certain kind, such as a *southern* stingray

spiracles (SPIR uh kulz) — the openings through which a ray draws water for breathing

A snorkeler peers down at a manta ray in clear tropical seas.

INDEX

FURTHER READING

Find out more about rays with these helpful books:
Ling, Mary. *Amazing Fish.* Knopf, 1991.
Taylor, David. *Animal Monsters.* Lerner, 1989.